ReadyGEN Text Collection

GRADE 2

PEARSON

Glenview, Illinois • Boston, Massachusetts • Chandler, Arizona • Hoboken, New Jersey

Cover: Dean MacAdam

Copyright © 2016 by Pearson Education, Inc. or its affiliates. All Rights Reserved. Printed in the United States of America. This publication is protected by copyright, and permission should be obtained from the publisher prior to any prohibited reproduction, storage in a retrieval system, or transmission in any form or by any means, electronic, mechanical, photocopying, recording, or otherwise. For information regarding permissions, request forms, and the appropriate contacts within the Pearson Education Global Rights & Permissions department, please visit www.pearsoned.com/permissions/.

Acknowledgments of third-party content appear on pages 172–173, which constitute an extension of this copyright page.

PEARSON, ALWAYS LEARNING, and READYGEN are exclusive trademarks owned by Pearson Education, Inc. or its affiliates in the U.S. and/or other countries.

Unless otherwise indicated herein, any third-party trademarks that may appear in this work are the property of their respective owners and any references to third-party trademarks, logos, or other trade dress are for demonstrative or descriptive purposes only. Such references are not intended to imply any sponsorship, endorsement, authorization, or promotion of Pearson's products by the owners of such marks, or any relationship between the owner and Pearson Education, Inc. or its affiliates, authors, licensees, or distributors.

ISBN-13: 978-0-328-85278-9
ISBN-10:   0-328-85278-3
5   16

Table of Contents

Unit 1 Understanding Communities

Unit 2 Making Decisions

Unit 3 Building Ideas

Acknowledgments

Snowshoe Hare's Winter Home

by Gillian Richardson   Art by Giuliano Ferri

Something cold tickled Snowshoe Hare on the nose. He looked up to see snowflakes tumbling and twirling. They carpeted the grassy clearing, coated the pine trees, and capped the rocks. Snowshoe Hare could hardly feel them dusting his fur. He leaped up to catch them on his tongue. Each one vanished before he could taste it.

"Quit fooling around," said Bear, ambling into the clearing. "Can't you feel how cold the air is? That's the signal. It's time to hibernate."

"What does that mean?" Snowshoe Hare asked, stopping to catch his breath.

" I find a place to sleep when winter comes,"
Bear said. "I won't come out again until it's warmer."

Snowshoe Hare didn't feel cold. Why should Bear,
with his thick fur coat, need to hide from winter?
"Where do you go?" Snowshoe Hare asked.

"Up in the hills. Got a cozy den all picked out."
Bear looked up at the heavy clouds and yawned.
"If I were you, I'd find a winter home, too.
See you in the spring."

Snowshoe Hare watched Bear lumber away. "Sleep?"
he asked. "That sounds boring." He hopped a few steps
and grinned at his own tracks on the snowy ground.
"I'd rather go exploring."

Near the pond, Snowshoe Hare met Beaver
cutting branches from a fallen poplar tree.

"Are you having lunch?" Snowshoe Hare asked.

"Nope. Gathering branches to take to the bottom
of my pond," Beaver answered.

" Why?" asked Snowshoe Hare.

" Those snow flurries are the signal that my pond will
soon freeze over. I'll have to stay in my lodge," Beaver
said, dragging a branch down the muddy slope of the pond.
" I can reach this food through my underwater tunnel.
You'd better store some food or you'll go hungry."

Snowshoe Hare watched Beaver and the branch sink
out of sight. "Who wants to spend all winter eating soggy
old branches?"

Water trickled out of Beaver's dam and became a stream. Snowshoe Hare hopped along its edge, nibbling juicy grass. He leaped back as cold water splashed him. Trout blew bubbles near the surface.

"Aren't you afraid the water will freeze?" Snowshoe Hare asked.

"Ice on top doesn't bother me. It's the signal to stay near the bottom where the water is warmer." Trout waved his fins. "Want to join me down below?"

Snowshoe Hare dipped a paw, then shook off the chilly drops. "I'd rather stay dry, thanks."

A lumpy shadow rose beneath Trout. A small head popped up. "Aren't you two paying attention to the signal? It's time to hibernate," said Turtle.

"But you already have your house on your back," Snowshoe Hare said.

"Won't keep the cold out. I'll snuggle into the mud at the bottom of Beaver's pond." Turtle sneezed a snowflake off her nose. "You'll need to keep warm, too."

Snowshoe Hare shrugged and thumped his foot. "I have to stay above the water. I couldn't breathe down there."

"Suit yourself," Turtle said. She crawled out of the stream and headed for the pond as snow covered her shell.

That evening the air crackled with cold. Snowshoe Hare saw Duck circling above the pond.

"I can't land. It's starting to freeze," Duck called down to Snowshoe Hare. "Happens every year about this time. It's the signal for me to get moving."

" Where are you going?" Snowshoe Hare asked.

"South. It's warmer there. I can't stay here if there's no open water. How would I get food from the bottom of the pond? Why don't you come along?" Duck said, spiraling upward.

Snowshoe Hare peered over his shoulder. "No wings!" he called out, but Duck was a tiny speck against the blue-green ribbons of northern lights dancing in the sky.

Alone, Snowshoe Hare watched the snow pile up all around. Winter had arrived, and his friends had disappeared. They all had places to go for the cold season.

"What am I going to do?" Snowshoe Hare wondered. "I don't want to sleep all winter like Bear. I can't stay under the ice like Beaver and Turtle and Trout. I can't fly away like Duck."

Just then, Snowshoe Hare heard some friendly voices: "Stay with us! We'll show you how to play hide-and-seek with Fox."

"Who's there?" Snowshoe Hare asked, peering through the flurries at three ghostly shapes.

"We don't hibernate or travel far away. We can dig through the snow for grass or snack on buds. We'll find a cozy bed in a snowbank. Hardly anyone will notice us."

"Where did you get your white coats?" asked Snowshoe Hare.

"Take a look at yourself!" they said and laughed.

Snowshoe Hare did. His coat was white, too! Bit by bit, his brown fur had changed when cold days signaled the coming winter.

"We're off!" the three snowshoe hares cried as they dashed off across the snowdrifts. "Come with us!"

Snowshoe Hare leaped high, then bounded along the trail left by their huge feet.

This was his winter home!

The
HOUSE
on
MAPLE
STREET

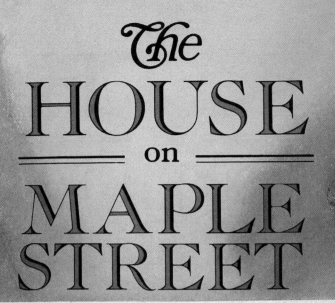

BONNIE PRYOR

illustrated by
BETH PECK

This is 107 Maple Street. Chrissy and Jenny live here with their mother and father, a dog named Maggie, and a fat cat named Sally.

Three hundred years ago there was no house here or even a street. There was only a forest and a bubbling spring where the animals came to drink.

One day a fierce storm roared across the forest. The sky rolled with thunder, and lightning crashed into a tree. A deer sniffed the air in alarm. Soon the woods were ablaze.

The next spring a few sturdy flowers poked
through the ashes, and by the year after that the
land was covered with grass. Some wildflowers
grew at the edge of the stream where the deer had
returned to drink.

One day the earth trembled, and a cloud of dust
rose to the sky. A mighty herd of buffalo had come
to eat the sweet grass and drink from the stream.

People came, following the buffalo herd. They set up their teepees near the stream, and because they liked it so much, they stayed for the whole summer.

One boy longed to be a great hunter like his father, but for now he could only pretend with his friends. In their games, one boy was chosen to be the buffalo.

His father taught the boy how to make an arrowhead and smooth it just so, the way his father had taught him. But the boy was young, and the day was hot.

He ran off to play with his friends and left the arrowhead on a rock. When he came back later to get it, he could not find it.

The buffalo moved on, searching for new grass, and the people packed up their tepees and followed.

For a long time the land was quiet. Some rabbits made their home in the stump of a burned tree, and a fox made a den in some rocks.

One day there was a new sound. The fox looked up. A wagon train passed by, heading for California. The settlers stopped beside the stream for a night. But they dreamed of gold and places far away and were gone the next morning.

Other wagons came, following the tracks of the first. The fox family moved into the woods, but the rabbits stayed snug in their burrows until the people had gone.

Soon after, a man and a woman camped along the stream. They were heading west, but the woman would soon have a child. They looked around them and knew it was a good place to stay. The man cut down trees and made a house.

He pulled up the tree stumps left from the fire and planted his crops. The child was a girl, and they named her Ruby and called her their little jewel.

Ruby had a set of china dishes that she played with every day. One day when she was making a mudpie on the banks of the stream, she found an arrowhead buried deep in the ground. She put it in a cup to show her father when he came in from the fields.

Ruby's mother called her to watch the new baby.
While she was gone, a rabbit sniffed at the cup
and knocked it off the rock. It fell into the tunnel
to his burrow, and the rabbit moved away to a new
home under the roots of a tree.

Ruby grew up and moved away, but her brother stayed on the farm. By now there were other people nearby, and he married a girl from another farm. They had six children, and he built a larger house so they would all fit.

Now the old wagon trail was used as a road, and the dust got into the house. When his wife complained, Ruby's brother planted a row of maple trees along the road to keep out the dust and shade the house. After the children were grown, he and his wife moved away, but one of their daughters stayed on the farm with her husband and children.

One day the children's great-aunt Ruby came for
a visit. She was an old lady with snow-white hair.
The children loved to hear her stories of long ago.
She told them about the cup and arrowhead she
had lost when she was a girl.

After she left, the children looked and looked.
But they never found them, though they searched
for days.

The town had grown nearly to the edge of the
farm, and another man up the road filled in the
stream and changed its course. For a while there
was a trickle of water in the spring when the snow
melted, but weeds and dirt filled in the bed, until
hardly anyone remembered a stream had ever
been there.

New people lived on the farm. It was the schoolteacher and his family, and they sold much of the land to others. The road was paved with bricks, so there was no longer any dust, but the maple trees remained. The branches hung down over the road, making it shady and cool. People called it Maple Street. Automobiles drove on the road, along with carts and wagons, and there were many new houses.

The house was crumbling and old, and one day some men tore it down. For a while again, the land was bare. The rabbits lived comfortably, with only an occasional owl or fox to chase them. But one day a young couple came walking along and stopped to admire the trees.

"What a wonderful place for a home," said the young woman. So they hired carpenters and masons to build a cozy house of red bricks with white trim.

The young couple lived happily in the house for several years. The young man got a job in another town, and they had to move.

The house was sold to a man and a woman who had two girls named Chrissy and Jenny and a dog named Maggie, and a fat cat named Sally.

The girls helped their father dig up a spot of ground for a garden, but it was Maggie the dog who dug up something white in the soft spring earth. "Stop," cried Chrissy, and she picked up the tiny cup made of china. Inside was the arrowhead found and lost so long ago.

"Who lost these?" the girls wondered. Chrissy
and Jenny put the cup and arrowhead on a shelf
for others to see. Someday perhaps their children
will play with the tiny treasures and wonder about
them, too. But the cup and arrowhead will forever
keep their secrets, and the children can only dream.

Pig

by Valerie Worth

The pig is bigger
Than we had thought
And not so pink,
Fringed with white
Hairs that look
Gray, because while
They say a pig is clean,
It is not always; still,
We like this huge, cheerful,
Rich, soft-bellied beast—
It wants to be comfortable,
And does not care much
How the thing is managed.

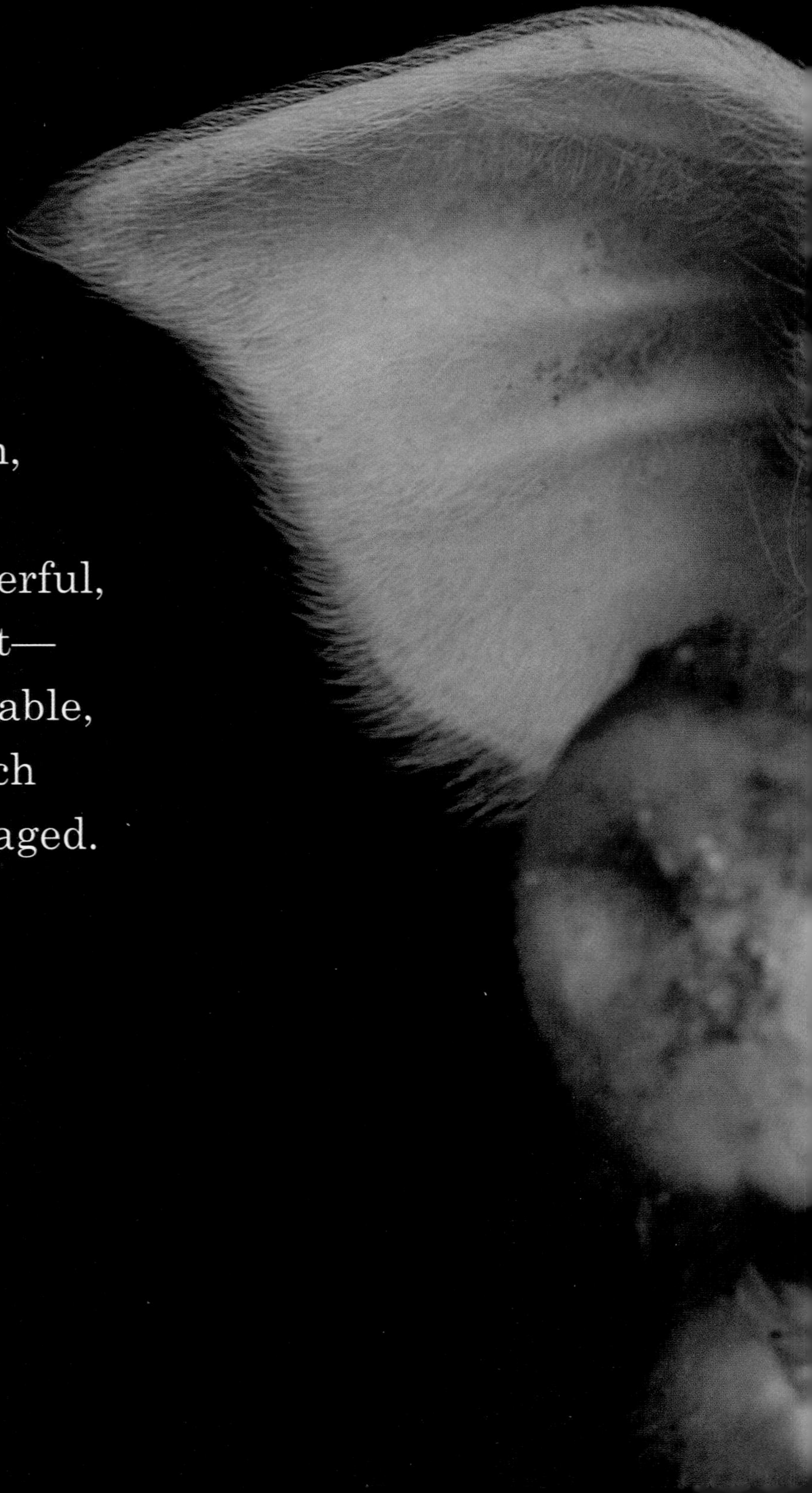

Something Told the Wild Geese

by Rachel Field

Something told the wild geese
   It was time to go.
Though the fields lay golden
   Something whispered,—'Snow.'
Leaves were green and stirring,
   Berries, luster-glossed,

But beneath warm feathers
   Something cautioned,—'Frost.'
All the sagging orchards
   Steamed with amber spice,
But each wild breast stiffened
   At remembered ice.
Something told the wild geese
   It was time to fly,—
Summer sun was on their wings,
   Winter in their cry.

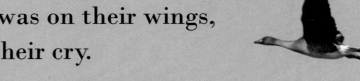

Subways Are People

by Lee Bennett Hopkins

Subways are people—

    People standing
    People sitting
    People swaying to and fro
    Some in suits
    Some in tatters
    People I will never know

    Some with glasses
    Some without
    Boy with smile
    Girl with frown

    People dashing
    Steel flashing
    Up and down and
    'round the town.

Subways are people—

    People old
    People new
    People always on the go
    Racing, running, rushing people
    People I will never know.

FISHING IN THE CREEK

by Linda Oatman High

Fishing in the creek,
seeking bites on my line,
I sigh,
hungry for a pan-fried trout.

Baited with mayfly and jig,
big earthworms squirming
in the bucket,
I cast behind a pine,
near my one-room school,
and the line squiggles
with a nibble.

I wait,
patient,
and then troll again.

When the pole bends,
I yank from my seat on the bank,
catching the fattest fish
in the creek,
stocked
just last week.

In the springtime sunlight,
the sleek trout shines—
shades of the rainbow,
eyes like jeweled fire.

I pray
the fish doesn't swim
away,
on this great April day.

A CHAIR FOR MY MOTHER

by Vera B. Williams

My mother works as a waitress in the Blue Tile Diner. After school sometimes I go to meet her there. Then her boss, Josephine, gives me a job too.

I wash the salts and peppers and fill the ketchups. One time I peeled all the onions for the onion soup. When I finish, Josephine says, "Good work, honey," and pays me. And every time, I put half of my money into the jar.

It takes a long time to fill a jar this big. Every day when my mother comes home from work, I take down the jar. My mama empties all her change from tips out of her purse for me to count. Then we push all of the coins into the jar.

Sometimes my mama is laughing when she comes home from work. Sometimes she's so tired she falls asleep while I count the money out into piles. Some days she has lots of tips. Some days she has only a little. Then she looks worried. But each evening every single shiny coin goes into the jar.

We sit in the kitchen to count the tips. Usually Grandma sits with us too. While we count, she likes to hum. Often she has money in her old leather wallet for us. Whenever she gets a good bargain on tomatoes or bananas or something she buys, she puts by the savings and they go into the jar.

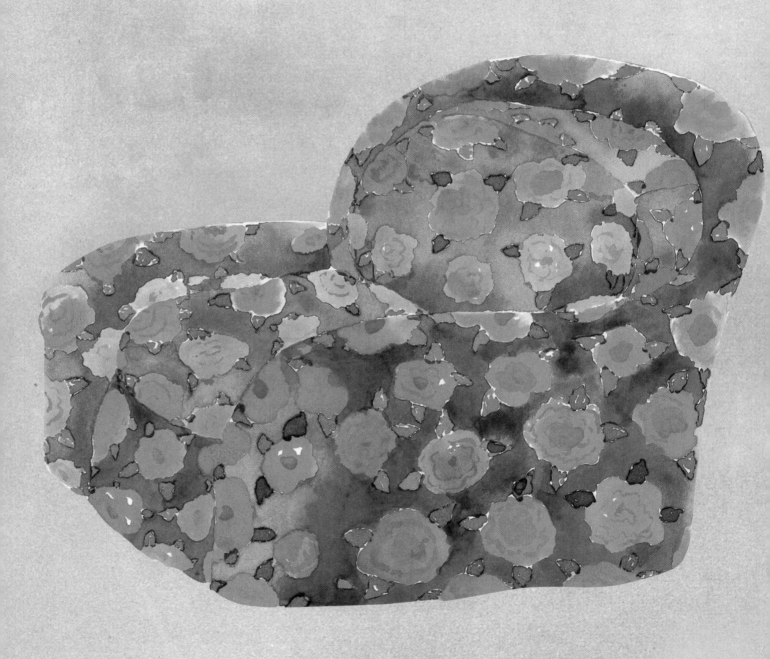

When we can't get a single other coin into the jar, we are going to take out all the money and go and buy a chair.

Yes, a chair: A wonderful, beautiful, fat, soft armchair. We will get one covered in velvet with roses all over it. We are going to get the best chair in the whole world.

That is because our old chairs burned up. There was a big fire in our other house. All our chairs burned. So did our sofa and so did everything else. That wasn't such a long time ago.

My mother and I were coming home from buying new shoes. I had new sandals. She had new pumps. We were walking to our house from the bus. We were looking at everyone's tulips. She was saying she liked red tulips and I was saying I liked yellow ones. Then we came to our block.

Right outside our house stood two big fire engines. I could see lots of smoke. Tall orange flames came out of the roof. All the neighbors stood in a bunch across the street. Mama grabbed my hand and we ran. My uncle Sandy saw us and ran to us. Mama yelled, "Where's Mother?" I yelled, "Where's my grandma?" My aunt Ida waved and shouted, "She's here, she's here. She's O.K. Don't worry."

Grandma was all right. Our cat was safe too, though it took a while to find her. But everything else in our whole house was spoiled.

What was left of the house was turned to charcoal and ashes.

We went to stay with my mother's sister Aunt Ida and Uncle Sandy. Then we were able to move into the apartment downstairs. We painted the walls yellow. The floors were all shiny. But the rooms were very empty.

The first day we moved in, the neighbors brought
pizza and cake and ice cream. And they brought a lot
of other things too.

The family across the street brought a table and
three kitchen chairs. The very old man next door
gave us a bed from when his children were little.

My other grandpa brought us his beautiful rug. My mother's other sister, Sally, had made us red and white curtains. Mama's boss, Josephine, brought pots and pans, silverware and dishes. My cousin brought me her own stuffed bear.

Everyone clapped when my grandma made a speech. "You are all the kindest people," she said, "and we thank you very, very much. It's lucky we're young and can start all over."

That was last year, but we still have no sofa and no big chairs. When Mama comes home, her feet hurt. "There's no good place for me to take a load off my feet," she says. When Grandma wants to sit back and hum and cut up potatoes, she has to get as comfortable as she can on a hard kitchen chair.

So that is how come Mama brought home the biggest jar she could find at the diner and all the coins started to go into the jar.

Now the jar is too heavy for me to lift down. Uncle Sandy gave me a quarter. He had to boost me up so I could put it in.

INFORMATION

70

After supper Mama and Grandma and I stood in front of the jar. "Well, I never would have believed it, but I guess it's full," Mama said.

My mother brought home little paper wrappers for the nickels and the dimes and the quarters. I counted them all out and wrapped them all up.

On my mother's day off, we took all the coins to the bank. The bank exchanged them for ten-dollar bills. Then we took the bus downtown to shop for our chair.

We shopped through four furniture stores. We tried out big chairs and smaller ones, high chairs and low chairs, soft chairs and harder ones. Grandma said she felt like Goldilocks in "The Three Bears" trying out all the chairs.

Finally we found the chair we were all dreaming of. And the money in the jar was enough to pay for it. We called Aunt Ida and Uncle Sandy. They came right down in their pickup truck to drive the chair home for us. They knew we couldn't wait for it to be delivered.

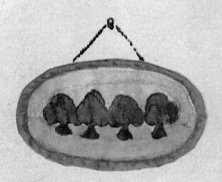

I tried out our chair in the back of the truck. Mama wouldn't let me sit there while we drove. But they let me sit in it while they carried it up to the door.

We set the chair right beside the window with the red and white curtains. Grandma and Mama and I all sat in it while Aunt Ida took our picture.

Now Grandma sits in it and talks with people going by in the daytime. Mama sits down and watches the news on TV when she comes home from her job. After supper, I sit with her and she can reach right up and turn out the light if I fall asleep in her lap.

I Wanna Iguana

BY KAREN KAUFMAN ORLOFF
ILLUSTRATED BY DAVID CATROW

Dear Mom,

I know you don't think I should have Mikey Gulligan's baby iguana when he moves, but here's why I should. If I don't take it, he goes to Stinky and Stinky's dog, Lurch, will eat it.

You don't want that to happen, do you?

Signed,
Your sensitive son,
Alex

Dear Alex,

I'm glad you're so compassionate, but
I doubt that Stinky's mother will let
Lurch get into the iguana's cage.

Nice try, though.

Love,
Mom

Dear Mom,

Did you know that iguanas are really quiet and they're cute too. I think they are much cuter than hamsters.

Love,
Your adorable son,
Alex

Dear Alex,
Tarantulas are quiet too, but I wouldn't want one as a pet. By the way, that iguana of Mikey's is uglier than Godzilla. Just thought I'd mention it.
Love,
Mom

Dear Mom,

You would never even have to see the iguana. I'll keep his cage in my room on the dresser next to my soccer trophies. Plus, he's so small, I bet you'll never even know he's there.

Love and a zillion and one kisses,
Alex

Dear Alex,

Iguanas can grow to be over six feet long. You won't have enough space in your whole room, much less on your dresser (with or without your trophies).

Love,
Mom

Dear Mom,

It takes 15 years for an iguana to get that big. Mikey told me. I'll be married by then and probably living in my own house.

Love,
Your smart and mature kid,
Alex

Dear Alex,

How are you going to get a girl to marry you when you own a six-foot-long reptile?

Love,
Your concerned mother

Dear Mom,
Forget the girl.
I need a new friend now!
This iguana can be the brother I've always wanted.

Love,
Your lonely child, Alex

Dear Alex,

You have a brother.

Love,
Mom

Dear Mom,

I know I have a brother but he's just a baby. What fun is that? If I had an iguana, I could teach it tricks and things. Ethan doesn't do tricks. He just burps.

Love,
Grossed-out Alex

Dear Alex,

How do I know you're ready for a pet? Remember what happened when you took home the class fish?

Love,
Mom

Dear Mom,

If I knew the fish was going to jump into the spaghetti sauce, I never would have taken the cover off the jar!

Love,
Your son who has learned his lesson

P.S. Iguanas don't like spaghetti.

Dear Alex,

Let's say I let you have the iguana on a trial basis. What exactly would you do to take care of it?

Love,
Mom

Dear Mom,

I would feed him every day (he eats lettuce). And I would make sure he had enough water. And I would clean his cage when it got messy.

Love, Responsible Alex

P.S. What's a trial basis?

Dear Alex,

A trial basis means Dad and I see how well you take care of him for a week or two before we decide if you can have him forever. Remember, Stinky and Lurch are waiting!

Love,
Mom

P.S. If you clean his cage as well as you clean your room, you're in trouble.

92

Dear Mom,

I'll really, really, really try to clean my room and the iguana's cage. Also, listen to this. I'll pay for the lettuce with my allowance. I mean, how much can one baby iguana eat anyway?

Love,
Alex the financial wizard

"Are you sure you want to do this, Alex?"

"Yes, Mom!
I wanna iguana. . .
Please!"

Dear Alex,
Look on your dresser.

Love,
Mom

94

"YESSSS!
Thank you!
Thank you!"

95

MONEY MATTERS

by Alan Katz

I saved all my pennies
and soon had a nickel.
I saved all my nickels
and soon had a dime.
I saved all my dimes
and soon had a quarter.
I saved all my quarters
and went to the store.

Yes, I'd saved and saved for a video system,
which really was quite an expense.
But the clerk looked down and laughed in
my face . . .

I only had eighty-three cents.

SHARING

by Shel Silverstein

I'll share your toys, I'll share your money,
I'll share your toast, I'll share your honey,
I'll share your milk and your cookies too—
The hard part's sharing mine with you.

Lizard Longing

by Tony Johnston
For Sam and for Tim Takeuchi

I'm gonna tell Mama
I want an iguana,
all blinky and scaly
just like a piranha.
I don't want some flora,
I'd rather have fauna.
I'm gonna tell Mama
I want an iguana.

Unfair

by Shel Silverstein

They don't allow pets in this apartment.
That's not decent, that's not fair.
They don't allow pets in this apartment.
They don't listen, they don't care.
I told them he's quiet and never does bark,
I told them he'd do all his stuff in the park,
I told them he's cuddly and friendly, and yet—
They won't allow pets.

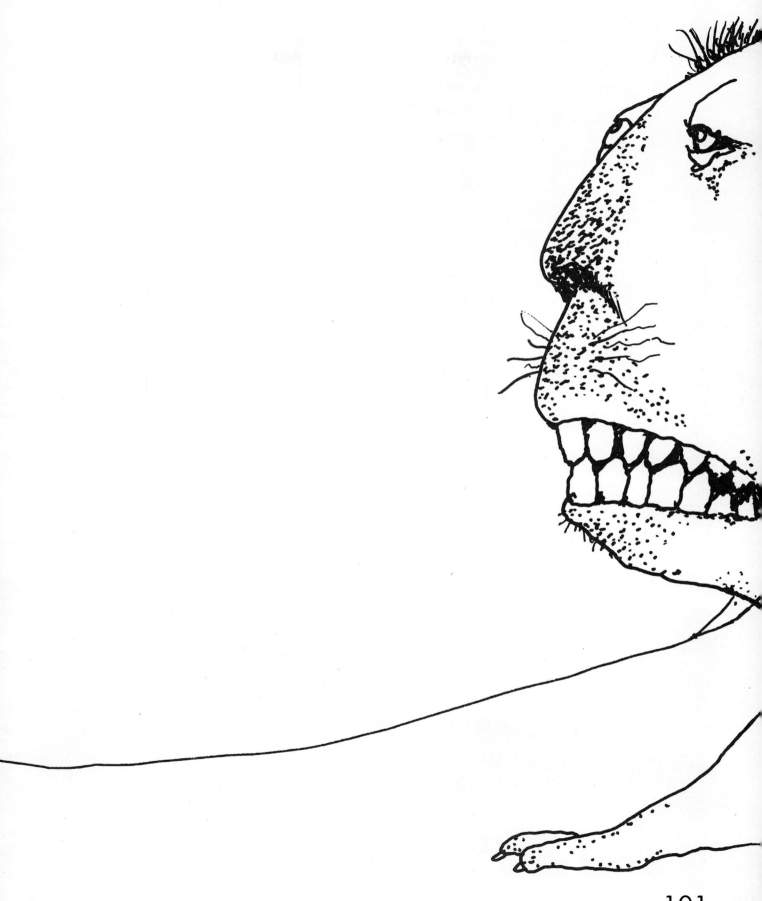

MARCHING
WITH AUNT SUSAN

Written by
Claire Rudolf Murphy

Illustrated by
Stacey Schuett

Papa took my brothers hiking, but not me.

"Strenuous exercise is not for girls, Bessie," he told me.

"You're not strong enough," Enie said.

"It's not ladylike," Charlie added.

"I can ride my bicycle faster than anyone on the block," I told my brothers. "Even you."

"Girls shouldn't ride bicycles either," Charlie said.

And they left without me.

Inside, Mama bustled around, preparing for a party.

"I'm strong enough to hike," I said. "Papa wouldn't take me along, just because I'm a girl."

"You can help me get ready for the suffrage tea," Mama said. "Aunt Mary will be arriving soon with our guest of honor, Miss Susan B. Anthony."

"Suffrage? I'm the one who's suffering." I picked up the newspaper and stared at Miss Anthony's photo. "She looks like a crabby old lady."

"A crabby old lady who has fought fifty years for women's rights," Mama said," even when people threw garbage at her and called her names."

At the tea, everybody swarmed around Miss Anthony. They called her Aunt Susan, even though they weren't related to her.

She spoke about the long fight for equal rights. She told us that children should grow up in a world where both men and women were free.

Later, Aunt Mary introduced me to Aunt Susan.

"Why can't girls do the same things as boys?" I asked her.

She shook her head. "When I was your age, my teacher thought only boys were smart enough to learn long division."

"That's not right," I said.

"Come to the rally in San Francisco tomorrow, Bessie. Women's votes can help change the world."

Golden Gate Auditorium was so crowded that I could barely breathe. Aunt Susan stood on a stage, surrounded by hundreds of roses. Her voice thundered across the hall. "The votes of all the people, including women with men, will surely bring about the wisest and best government the world has ever seen."

I pulled a white handkerchief out of my purse and joined the sea of flags waving in the air.

The day after the rally, I rode my bicycle over to my best friend Rita's house. "You should have heard Aunt Susan speak yesterday," I told her.

"My papa says ladies shouldn't speak in public," Rita said.

"Aunt Susan says that girls are just as smart as boys. We should get to help make decisions too."

"Papa decides everything in our family," Rita said.

"That's not right." I looked at my best friend. "Someday I want to vote. Let's see if we can help out at suffrage headquarters."

All through the summer, Rita and I wrote letters, licked envelopes, and painted posters. As we worked, we listened to women talk.

"Men decide everything. They even decide if we should get to vote."

"Men decide how the children are raised."

"Men decide how the household money is spent."

"I don't understand," I said to Rita. "I get to spend my allowance any way I want. And Mama makes decisions about lots of our purchases."

"Not at our house." Rita shook her head. "Papa keeps track of every penny."

The week before the election, we visited a factory in San Francisco. Rows and rows of girls sat hunched over, sewing in a dark room. Aunt Susan encouraged them to come to our suffrage parade.

Afterward, a girl walked up. "Me and my sister did some extra sewing to help the campaign." She handed Aunt Susan two dimes. "If women win the vote, will I be able to go to school?"

I couldn't imagine not learning how to read and write. I leaned against the wall and tried to catch my breath.

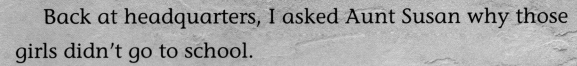

Back at headquarters, I asked Aunt Susan why those girls didn't go to school.

"Many parents can't make enough money to feed their families," she told me. "So the children have to work."

"Can women getting the vote change that?" I asked.

Aunt Susan nodded. "We can work to pass laws that will help adults *and* children."

I dumped out all the coins in my purse and handed them to her. "If those girls can give money, I should too."

Later I painted a picture of the factory girl on a banner for the parade. Rita printed the letters.

Sunday afternoon before the vote, Rita, Mama, and I marched along, carrying our banner. The crowd cheered as we sang new lyrics to "My Country, 'Tis of Thee."

Our country, now from thee,
Claim we our liberty,
In freedom's name.
Guarding home's altar fires,
Daughters of patriot sires,
Their zeal our own inspires,
Justice to claim.

But then men began shouting. "Women belong in the kitchen! Girls belong at home!"

Rita's father appeared and dragged her away. "No daughter of mine will parade in the streets!"

A boy splattered an egg down the front of my white dress. "What do you want to be—a man?" he yelled.

I stood frozen, watching the oozing yellow stain spread, until Mama picked up Rita's end of the banner and we marched on.

When he heard what had happened, Papa bought me a new white dress. If only it was that easy to win the election.

Monday after school, Mama and I stood at the ferry launch and held up a new sign.

**REMEMBER YOUR DAUGHTERS—VOTE
YES on REFERENDUM #6**

I couldn't tell if I got more pats on the head or grumbles from the men walking by. But Mama said, "It only matters how they vote tomorrow."

The day after the election, my brothers raced me home from school. Charlie grabbed the newspaper off the front porch.

"Women Lose the Vote!" he shouted.

I leaned my bicycle against the house and snatched the newspaper out of his hand.

"What are you so mad about?" asked Enie.

"Someday you'll get to vote and you don't even care. Mama is as smart as Papa, and I'm as smart as you. We should get to vote too."

Mama came out and picked up my bicycle. "Aunt Susan says that a bicycle gives a woman freedom. Teach me how to ride, Bessie."

"It's hard to do," I said, sitting down on the steps.

"When you first tried to ride, you kept falling and scraping your knees," she reminded me. "But you didn't give up."

Finally I showed her what to do—how to mount the bicycle, balance, pedal, and drag her feet to stop.

When Papa arrived home, Mama was wobbling up and down the street. "I'm sorry about the election, Bessie," he said.

"Girls should be allowed to do the same things as boys, Papa."

"Why don't we go hiking this Saturday?" he asked.

"Thanks, Papa," I said, grabbing his hand. "And Sunday there's a rally for the next suffrage campaign. Come march with Mama and me."

Ever since I learned that women first won the vote in the Western states, I have been fascinated with the seventy-two-year struggle for American women's suffrage. I realized that I had never read about women's suffrage in my college history courses, so I set out to learn all I could. I wanted to find a real girl to write about, and eventually I found the Keith-McHenry-Pond Family Papers at The Bancroft Library at the University of California, Berkeley. Inside boxes and cartons were Bessie's journals, newspaper articles about her family's hiking, and the suffrage collection of her aunt, Mary McHenry Keith. My hands shook as I read letters from my hero Susan B. Anthony to Aunt Mary.

Marching with Aunt Susan is based on actual events in the 1896 campaign. The quote from Susan B. Anthony's speech at Golden Gate Auditorium was one she often used. The version of "My Country, 'Tis of Thee" that Bessie sings in the parade was written by Elizabeth Harnett and performed at suffrage meetings around the country.

This story is my chance to march with Aunt Susan and to thank her, Bessie, Aunt Mary, and the hundreds of thousands of women who won the vote for me and for you.

BESSIE

Bessie Keith Pond was a real girl who lived in Berkeley, California, in 1896. She had two older brothers, Enie (Enoch) and Charlie. Her father Charles was a naval commander. Her mother Emma was a painter and poet, who invented the board game Constitution.

Bessie grew up in a family of avid suffragists: her grandmother, mother, and especially her aunt, Mary McHenry Keith, who was a leader in both California campaigns.

Aunt Mary was the first California woman to graduate from law school and the wife of the well-known landscape painter William Keith. She became close friends with Susan B. Anthony during her 1895 and 1896 trips to California. In 1905, when Anthony returned for one last trip to California, Uncle Willie painted her portrait.

Bessie wrote poetry and taught art and music all her life. For many years, Bessie, her father, and her brothers took month-long mountain hikes and snowshoe trips in the Sierra Nevada mountains, sometimes up to 300 miles. This was so unusual that the family was often featured in the newspaper. An article in the June 24, 1927, edition of the *San Francisco Call* described Bessie as an "athletic girl with a fondness for outdoor life."

(1886-1955)

KEITH POND

CALIFORNIA SUFFRAGE CAMPAIGN

In 1895, the California legislature agreed to let men vote on an amendment to the state constitution in support of women's suffrage. That year Susan B. Anthony traveled to California to help get the referendum on the ballot and returned in May 1896 to lead the campaign for the November election.

Hundreds of suffragists across the state organized meetings in every town. Anthony spoke up to thirty times a day at picnics, schools, factories, military encampments, farmers' markets, church conventions, labor meetings, women and men's clubs, and even poolrooms. Women and girls worked at headquarters around the state, and working women stopped by after work to donate money or take home an armload of circulars to fold and address at night. Rallies and tea parties like the ones in the story took place from May through November, along with dinner parties, including one at the Keith home, which Anthony attended.

Ten days before the election, bar owners became worried that women's suffrage could mean passage of a law ending the sale of liquor. They quickly helped register thousands of men and instructed them to vote no.

The final tally was 247,454 votes: 110,355 for; 137,099 against.

The next morning Anthony said, "I don't care for myself. I am used to defeat, but these dear California women who have worked hard, how can they bear it?"

For many years, the suffrage movement languished in California and across America. In 1911, suffragists finally got a referendum back on the California ballot. Young suffragists campaigned in the newly invented automobile and used the telephone to reach voters. On October 10, 1911, fifteen years after the events depicted in this book, California became the sixth and largest state to approve women's suffrage.

Susan B. Anthony

(1820-1906)

Susan B. Anthony was raised as a Quaker with the belief that men and women are equal. But all around her she witnessed inequality. Girls who worked at her father's mill couldn't attend school because their families needed their wages. She and the other girls at her school weren't allowed to learn long division.

Later when she became a teacher, she earned only one-quarter the salary of male teachers. All these experiences made her want to work for change.

When Anthony was eighteen years old, she joined the abolitionist movement after hearing Lucretia Mott speak out against slavery. In 1851, she met Elizabeth Cady Stanton and became devoted to the cause of women's suffrage. Anthony believed that if women could vote, they could help pass laws to end slavery and to improve working conditions and the lives of the poor.

For more than fifty years Susan B. Anthony led the fight for women's suffrage along with her friend Elizabeth Cady Stanton. While Stanton wrote speeches and raised a family, Anthony campaigned across the country. She first visited California in 1871 and returned several times, including eight months during the campaign depicted in this book.

Even in her later years, Anthony was described as tireless, working night and day. At a celebration of her eighty-sixth birthday at the 1906 meeting of the National American Women's Suffrage Association, Susan proclaimed her famous rallying cry, "Failure is impossible."

In 1896, one woman reporter said she didn't believe in suffrage—until she interviewed Anthony.

'I WISH I WERE SUSAN B. ANTHONY," SHE WROTE. "THERE IS SOMETHING LOVEABLE IN HER FACE AND VOICE. SHE IS BEAUTIFUL IN HER PLAINNESS AND HER SMILE IS NOT TO BE FORGOTTEN."

Susan B. Anthony died in Rochester on March 13, 1906. Memorial services were held all over the country, including one in San Francisco, during which William Keith's portrait of her was unveiled.

After Anthony's death, Bessie's aunt, Mary McHenry Keith, and many other supporters around the country lobbied to make her birthday a national holiday. That never happened. But a dollar coin features her likeness.

Susan B. Anthony died before all American women won the vote in 1920, one hundred years after her birth. But her name is forever linked with the long battle for women's suffrage.

"Failure is impossible."

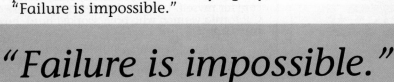

1787	U.S. Constitution leaves voting rights up to the states to decide. Only New Jersey allows women to vote, and only between 1776 and 1807.
1866	Elizabeth Cady Stanton and Susan B. Anthony form the American Equal Rights Association, an organization for white and black women and men dedicated to the goal of universal suffrage.
1869	Wyoming Territorial legislature grants full voting rights to women.
1870	Utah Territorial legislature grants full voting rights to women.
1870	The Fifteenth Amendment allows men of color to vote, but not women.
1872	Susan B. Anthony attempts to vote in the presidential election and is arrested.
1883	Washington Territorial legislature grants full voting rights to women.
1890	Wyoming is the first state to grant full voting rights to women.
1893	Colorado state referendum grants full voting rights to women.
1896	Utah and Idaho grant full voting rights to women. Suffrage referendum defeated in California.
1906	Susan B. Anthony dies.
1910	Washington state referendum grants full voting rights to women.
1911	California state referendum grants full voting rights to women.
1912	Oregon, Kansas, and Arizona grant full voting rights to women.
1913	Alaska Territorial Legislature grants full voting rights to women.
1914	Montana and Nevada grant full voting rights to women.
1918	South Dakota and Oklahoma referenda grant full voting rights to women.
1919	U.S. House of Representatives and Senate approve the Nineteenth Amendment granting all American women full voting rights.
1920	The Nineteenth Amendment wins the necessary two-thirds ratification from state legislatures.

Suffrage History

Our Constitution states that citizens should be allowed to vote, but it doesn't spell out who is considered to be a citizen. That was left up to each state to decide. In the early days of our country, only male landowners were allowed to vote. Men of color won the right to vote with passage of the Fifteenth Amendment in 1870, but women still could not vote.

Beginning with the first suffrage convention in Seneca Falls, New York, in 1848, women in every state worked to get the vote. The seventy-two-year campaign stretched through two wars and sixteen presidents. It included 56 state referendum campaigns, 480 campaigns to get legislatures to consider suffrage amendments, 47 campaigns for constitutional conventions, 277 campaigns directed at state party conventions, and 30 campaigns to get national parties to put suffrage in their platforms.

In 1878, the Susan B. Anthony amendment was first introduced in Congress. But it wasn't until 1919 that it finally passed both houses of Congress. In August 1920, Tennessee became the thirty-sixth state to ratify the Nineteenth Amendment. One hundred years after Susan B. Anthony's birth, women from every state finally gained the vote.

THE NINETEENTH AMENDMENT TO THE UNITED STATES CONSTITUTION

THE RIGHT OF CITIZENS OF THE UNITED STATES TO VOTE SHALL NOT BE DENIED OR ABRIDGED BY THE UNITED STATES OR BY ANY STATE ON ACCOUNT OF SEX.

CONGRESS SHALL HAVE THE POWER TO ENFORCE THIS ARTICLE BY APPROPRIATE LEGISLATION.

"Yes, I'll tell you what I think of bicycling. I think it has done more to emancipate women than anyone thing in the world. I rejoice every time I see a woman ride by on a wheel. It gives her a feeling of freedom and self-reliance."
—Susan B. Anthony (1896)

City Green

DyAnne DiSalvo-Ryan

There used to be a building right here on this lot. It was three floors up and down, an empty building nailed up shut for as long as I could remember. My friend Miss Rosa told me Old Man Hammer used to live there—some other neighbors too. But when I asked him about that, he only hollered, "Scram."

Old Man Hammer, hard as nails.

Last year two people from the city came by, dressed in suits and holding papers. They said, "This building is unsafe. It will have to be torn down."

By winter a crane with a wrecking ball was parked outside. Mama gathered everyone to watch from our front window. In three slow blows that building was knocked into a heap of pieces. Then workers took the rubble away in a truck and filled the hole with dirt.

Now this block looks like a big smile with one tooth missing. Old Man Hammer sits on his stoop and shakes his head. "Look at that piece of junk land on a city block," Old Man Hammer says. "Once that building could've been saved. But nobody even tried."

And every day when I pass this lot it makes me sad to see it. Every single day.

Then spring comes, and right on schedule
Miss Rosa starts cleaning her coffee cans.
Miss Rosa and I keep coffee cans outside our
windowsills. Every year we buy two packets
of seeds at the hardware store—sometimes
marigolds, sometimes zinnias, and one time
we tried tomatoes. We go to the park, scoop
some dirt, and fill up the cans halfway.

This time Old Man Hammer stops us on the way to the park. "This good for nothin' lot has plenty of dirt right here," he says.

Then all at once I look at Miss Rosa. And she is smiling back at me.

"A lot of dirt," Miss Rosa says.

"Like one big coffee can," I say.

That's when we decide to do something about this lot.

Quick as a wink I'm digging away, already thinking of gardens and flowers. But Old Man Hammer shakes his finger. "You can't dig more dirt than that. This lot is city property."

Miss Rosa and I go to see Mr. Bennett. He used to work for the city. "I seem to remember a program," he says, "that lets people rent empty lots."

That's how Miss Rosa and I form a group of people from our block. We pass around a petition that says: WE WANT TO LEASE THIS LOT. In less than a week we have plenty of names.

"Sign with us?" I ask Old Man Hammer.

"I'm not signin' nothin'," he says. "And nothin' is what's gonna happen."

But something did.

The next week, a bunch of us take a bus to city hall. We walk up the steps to the proper office and hand the woman our list. She checks her files and types some notes and makes some copies. "That will be one dollar, please."

We rent the lot from the city that day. It was just as simple as that.

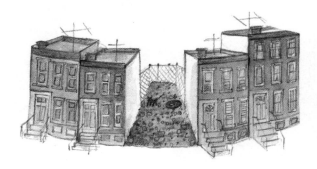

Saturday morning
I'm up with the sun and
looking at this lot. My
mama looks out too.
"Marcy," she says, and
hugs me close. "Today I'm
helping you and Rosa."

After shopping, Mama
empties her grocery bags
and folds them flat to carry
under her arm. "Come on,
Mrs. B.," Mama tells her
friend. "We're going to clear
this lot."

Then what do you know
but my brother comes
along. My brother is tall
and strong. At first, he
scratches his neck and
shakes his head just like
Old Man Hammer. But
Mama smiles and says,
"None of that here!" So
all day long he piles junk
in those bags and carries
them to the curb.

Now, this time of day is early. Neighbors pass by and see what we're doing. Most say, "We want to help too." They have a little time to spare. Then this one calls that one and that one calls another.

"Come on and help," I call to Old Man Hammer.

"I'm not helpin' nobody," he hollers. "You're all wastin' your time."

Sour grapes my mama'd say, and sour grapes is right.

Just before supper, when we are good and hungry, my mama looks around this lot. "Marcy," she says, "you're making something happen here."

Next day the city drops off tools like rakes and brooms, and a Dumpster for trash. Now there's even more neighbors to help. Miss Rosa, my brother, and I say "Good morning" to Old Man Hammer, but Old Man Hammer just waves like he's swatting a fly.

"Why is Old Man Hammer so mean and cranky these days?" my brother asks.

"Maybe he's really sad," I tell him. "Maybe he misses his building."

"That rotten old building?" My brother shrugs. "He should be happy the city tore down that mess." "Give him time," Miss Rosa says.

"Good things take time."

Mr. Bennett brings wood—old slats he's saved—and nails in a cup. "I knew all along I saved them for something," he says. "This wood's good wood."

Then Mr. Rocco from two houses down comes, carrying two cans of paint. "I'll never use these," he says. "The color's too bright. But here, this lot could use some brightening up."

Well, anyone can tell with all the excitement that something is going on. And everyone has an idea about what to plant—strawberries, carrots, lettuce, and more. Tulips and daisies, petunias, and more! Sonny turns the dirt over with a snow shovel. Even Leslie's baby tries to dig with a spoon.

For lunch, Miss Rosa brings milk and jelly and bread and spreads a beach towel where the junk is cleared. By the end of the day a fence is built and painted as bright as the sun.

Later, Mama kisses my cheek and closes my bedroom door. By the streetlights I see Old Man Hammer come down his steps to open the gate and walk to the back of this lot. He bends down quick, sprinkling something from his pocket and covering it over with dirt.

In the morning I tell my brother. "Oh, Marcy," he says. "You're dreaming. You're wishing too hard."

But I know what I saw, and I tell my mama, "Old Man Hammer's planted some seeds."

Right after breakfast, I walk to the back of this lot. And there it is—a tiny raised bed of soil. It is neat and tidy, just like the rows we've planted. Now I know for sure that Old Man Hammer planted something. So I pat the soil for good luck and make a little fence to keep the seeds safe.

Every day I go for a look inside our garden lot. Other neighbors stop in too. One day Mrs. Wells comes by. "This is right where my grandmother's bedroom used to be," she says. "That's why I planted my flowers there."

I feel sad when I hear that. With all the digging and planting and weeding and watering, I'd forgotten about the building that had been on this lot. Old Man Hammer had lived there too. I go to the back, where he planted his seeds. I wonder if this was the place where his room used to be.

I look down. Beside my feet, some tiny stems are sprouting. Old Man Hammer's seeds have grown! I run to his stoop. "Come with me!" I beg, tugging at his hand. "You'll want to see."

I walk him past the hollyhocks, the daisies, the peppers, the rows of lettuce. I show him the strawberries that I planted. When Old Man Hammer sees his little garden bed, his sour grapes turn sweet. "Marcy, child." He shakes his head. "This lot was good for nothin'. Now it's nothin' but good," he says.

Soon summertime comes, and this lot really grows. It fills with vegetables, herbs, and flowers. And way in the back, taller than anything else, is a beautiful patch of yellow sunflowers. Old Man Hammer comes every day. He sits in the sun, eats his lunch, and sometimes comes back with supper.

Nobody knows how the sunflowers came— not Leslie, my brother, or Miss Rosa. Not Mr. Bennett, or Sonny, or anyone else. But Old Man Hammer just sits there smiling at me. We know whose flowers they are.

LINCOLN

by Nancy Byrd Turner

There was a boy of other days,
A quiet, awkward, earnest lad,
Who trudged long weary miles to get
A book on which his heart was set—
And then no candle had!

He was too poor to buy a lamp
But very wise in woodmen's ways.
He gathered seasoned bough and stem,
And crisping leaf, and kindled them
Into a ruddy blaze.

Then as he lay full length and read,
The firelight flickered on his face,
And etched his shadow on the gloom.
And made a picture in the room,
In that most humble place.

The hard years came, the hard years went,
But, gentle, brave, and strong of will,
He met them all. And when to-day
We see his pictured face, we say,
"There's light upon it still."

My America

by Jan Spivey Gilchrist

Have you seen my country?
Seen my magic skies?
Seen my mighty waters?
Have you seen my land?

Have you seen my country?
Seen my wings abound?
Seen my water creatures?
Seen my beasts and fowl?

Have you seen my people?
We hail from every shore.
Have you seen my homeland?
Have you seen my country?
Have you seen my AMERICA?

CITY TREES

by Edna St. Vincent Millay

The trees along this city street,
    Save for the traffic and the trains,
Would make a sound as thin and sweet
    As trees in country lanes.

And people standing in their shade
    Out of a shower, undoubtedly
Would hear such music as is made
    Upon a country tree.

Oh, little leaves that are so dumb
    Against the shrieking city air,
I watch you when the wind has come,—
    I know what sound is there.

Poems from Cricket Never Does

by Myra Cohn Livingston

Pines, tamed by fences,
pop their heads over to look
out at the traffic . . .

Wild branches, spilling
over the concrete wall, reach
out to touch the bus . . .

Illustrations

Photographs